QuoteOctopus.com

The best quotes

Publisher Contact

257 Swanston Street, Melbourne, VIC, AUSTRALIA

Email: hello@quoteoctopus.com

Social media: facebook.com/quoteoctopus

Acknowledgements

The team at Quote Octopus would like to thank our friends, family, suppliers and customers for making our vision of creating the highest-quality books a reality. Thanks for purchasing and enjoy the quotes!

This page is intentionally left blank

This page is intentionally left blank

And I think that being able to make people laugh and write a book that's funny makes the information go down a lot easier and it makes it a lot more fun to read, easier to understand, and often stronger. So there's all kinds of advantages to it.

Al Franken

Antitrust law isn't about protecting competing businesses from each other, it's about protecting competition itself on behalf of the public.

Al Franken

Anybody who deliberately propagandizes with lies should be held up to scorn and ridicule.

Al Franken

Apple has long been a leading innovator of mobile technology; I myself own an iPhone.

Al Franken

Armed with nothing more than a Facebook user's phone number and home address, anyone with an Internet connection and a few dollars can obtain personal information they should never have access to, including a user's date of birth, e-mail address, or estimated income.

Al Franken

As a source of innovation, an engine of our economy, and a forum for our political discourse, the Internet can only work if it's a truly level playing field. Small businesses should have the same ability to reach customers as powerful corporations. A blogger should have the same ability to find an audience as a media conglomerate.

Al Franken

As someone who's spent time with our troops in Iraq and Afghanistan on USO tours and met wounded warriors at Walter Reed and Bethesda, I feel a deep obligation to the men and women who have risked life and limb on our behalf.

Al Franken

At 'SNL,' I wrote political stuff, but I never felt the show should have an axe to grind. But when I left in '95, I could let my own beliefs out.

Al Franken

Bill Clinton is the greatest president of the 20th century because I played touch football with him.

Al Franken

Bob Dole used to be really funny. Barney Frank can be kind of funny. Bob Kerrey has a good sense of humor.

Al Franken

But in the right-wing media, they do have a right-wing bias. And they also have an agenda. So their agenda is: we're an adjunct of the Republican Party, and we're going push that agenda every day, and, as you say, brand these stories that help further the right-wing cause.

Al Franken

Call-time has renewed my faith in the need for public financing of elections. 'Call-time' is where I as the candidate, sit in a room with my 'call-time manager,' and a phone. Then I call people and ask them for money. For hours. Apparently, I'm really good at it.

Al Franken

Changing technologies, changing marketplaces, and even changing trends in anti-competitive practices have all presented challenges to antitrust enforcement.

Al Franken

Comedy to the Senate? Well, there certainly hasn't been a satirist or a political satirist who's done that. So, that really was uncharted territory during the campaign. But I think it's a good thing. Some people thought that it was an odd career arc, but to me it made absolute sense.

Al Franken

Demagoguery sells. And therefore radio stations will put it on. But that doesn't mean that you can't do something else and also make it sell. You know, when I look at an Ann Coulter or I look at a Rush or I look at a Sean Hannity, I think to myself, 'What kind of self-image do you have?'

Al Franken

Demagoguery sells. And therefore, radio stations will put it on. But that doesn't mean that you can't do something else and also make it sell.

Al Franken

During Vietnam, I was in college, enjoying my student deferment. The government wisely felt that, in my case, military service was less important than completing my studies to prepare me for my chosen career: comedian.

Al Franken

For 35 years, I was a writer. I wrote a lot of jokes. Some of them weren't funny. Some of them weren't appropriate. Some of them were downright offensive. I understand that.

Al Franken

Gary Bauer is a very good - he's a good friend of mine.

Al Franken

Google's screen for privacy settings does give you more options for what you share than Apple's does. But it's not a complete list, and people aren't aware of whether or not that information will go to a third party.

Al Franken

Grown-up love means actually understanding what you love, taking the good with the bad and helping your loved one grow. Love takes attention and work and is the best thing in the world.

Al Franken

Harvard's Kennedy School of Government asked me to serve as a fellow at its Shorenstein Center on the Press, Politics, and Public Policy. After my varied and celebrated career in television, movies, publishing, and the lucrative world of corporate speaking, being a fellow at Harvard seemed, frankly, like a step down.

Al Franken

Having an actual income can expand your romantic horizons toward the more appealing end of the spectrum.

Al Franken

Humor and seriousness are not in opposition to each other.

Al Franken

I also focus on Bush and his administration - who do a lot of lying - and how a right-wing media has allowed them to get away with a lot of stuff that, in a different media environment, they probably wouldn't be able to get away with.

Al Franken

I am a Minnesotan, and not just because I root for the Vikings and the Twins. I like the Minnesota-nice sensibility. I like the liberal tradition; I like the Hubert Humphrey tradition fighting for civil rights.

Al Franken

I ask the American people not to fall victim to disinformation. There are no death panels. The Affordable Care Act cuts the deficit.

Al Franken

I believe in not attacking a country pre-emptively unless you're sure of what you're doing and you're working with allies.

Al Franken

I believe people have a right to know what's going on with their information and how it's collected, how it's stored and who gets it.

Al Franken

I couldn't think of anything less appealing than molding the minds of tomorrow's leaders.

Al Franken

I do have a self-censor; everybody does, or at least most who are not pathological do.

Al Franken

I do personal attacks only on people who specialize in personal attacks.

Al Franken

I don't consider myself an artist necessarily, but craftsmen or people in the arts, their spiritualism is sort of when you're writing well or performing well or doing whatever you do well, there's an element of that that's either God-given, a talent that you're not necessarily responsible for.

Al Franken

I don't know how many of you have been to New York, but if a building is two blocks away from anything, you can't see it.

Al Franken

I don't know what happens to you after you die. I'm not banking on there being, like, a heaven.

Al Franken

I don't think I'm an angry person. I think I'm a person who's angry. I'm angry at the Bush administration; I'm angry at the right wing media. And by that I don't mean the media is right wing. I mean, there is a part of the media that's not the mainstream media. That's Fox, that is 'The Wall Street Journal' editorial page.

Al Franken

I felt like the luckiest kid in the world. And I was. I was growing up middle-class in a time when growing up middle-class in America meant there would be jobs for my parents, good schools for me to prepare myself for a career, and, if I worked hard and played by the rules, a chance for me to do anything I wanted.

Al Franken

I get satisfaction when I write something I like, when I'm happy with it.

Al Franken

I got interested in politics during the civil rights movement and then Vietnam.

Al Franken

I grew up in Minnesota, where we treasure our tradition of civic engagement - and our record of having the nation's highest voter participation.

Al Franken

I hope you realize, in a democracy, laughter is assent.

Al Franken

I just can't sit still and meditate; that doesn't kind of work for me. I don't even know exactly what it means.

Al Franken

I know I have an awful lot to learn from the people of Minnesota.

Al Franken

I know that it's probably not a good idea for a comedian, especially a satirist, to support a public policy group or a politician. This is something I learned only too well years ago when I did a fundraiser for Pol Pot. A few years later I saw 'The Killing Fields,' and I've got to tell you, I just felt like a schmuck.

Al Franken

I listen to NPR when I listen to the radio, but I don't listen to the radio that much. You know, I listen to Garrison Keillor, I listen to 'Prairie Home Companion.'

Al Franken

I once asked the most fabulous couple I know, Madonna and Guy Ritchie, how they kept things fresh despite having been married for almost seven months. 'It's a job, Al,' Guy told me. 'We work at it every day.'

Al Franken

I think Clinton fatigue was a real thing. It's just hard to get comfortable with Gore - it was hard for him to project who he is, the person people know in private.

Al Franken

I think Hell exists on Earth. It's a psychological state, or it can be a physical state. People who have severe mental illness are in Hell. People who have lost a loved one are in Hell. I think there are all kinds of different hells. It's not a place you go to after you die.

Al Franken

I think that the default for collecting any kind of personal data should be opt-in consent.

Al Franken

I think the Internet has developed at this incredibly rapid pace because of net neutrality, because of the free nature of it, because a YouTube can start the way YouTube started.

Al Franken

I think the government has a role in protecting the fundamental rights of its citizens.

Al Franken

I want to reclaim 'liberal.' I'm a liberal, and I think most Americans are liberals.

Al Franken

I'm a bit of a shill for the Clinton Administration, which has its perks. I'm invited to all the inaugural balls.

Al Franken

I'm crushed by the responsibility of writing a satirical book.

Al Franken

I'm for Israel's right to exist.

Al Franken

I'm from the Vietnam generation. I didn't serve.

Al Franken

I'm part of the mushball middle. I consider 'confused' the majority position because, thankfully, most people would rather be uncertain some of the time than 100% positive all the time - even when they're wrong.

Al Franken

I'm sure I've devoted enough thought to Rush Limbaugh for one lifetime.

Al Franken

I'm the New York Jew who actually grew up in Minnesota.

Al Franken

I've never understood why we would want to deny all the joys - and the challenges - of marriage to anyone. Which is why I think any loving, committed couple - gay or straight - should be able to get married.

Al Franken

I've spent my entire career being a satirist.

Al Franken

If 98 out of 100 doctors tell me I've got a problem, I should take their advice. And if those two other doctors get paid by Big Snack Food, like certain climate deniers get paid by Big Coal, I shouldn't take their advice.

Al Franken

If I put myself on the ballot and even 50 people voted for me, it'd be a travesty.

Al Franken

If Republicans eliminate Medicare, America will become a country in which you can never retire - and once you physically can no longer work, you are desperately poor until you die.

Al Franken

If someone hacks your password, you can change it - as many times as you want. You can't change your fingerprints. You have only ten of them. And you leave them on everything you touch; they are definitely not a secret.

Al Franken

If someone hacks your password, you can change it - as many times as you want.

Al Franken

If we have George W. Bush as president, we're going to go back to the kind of policies we had when his father and Ronald Reagan were president.

Al Franken

If you hear, day after day, liberals are rooting against armed forces, that is eventually going to have an effect on soldiers and troops who are actually going to believe that and it's wrong. It's just wrong.

Al Franken

If you look at terrorists, they really have no sense of humor.

Al Franken

If you use Facebook - as I do - Facebook in all likelihood has a unique digital file of your face, one that can be as accurate as a fingerprint and that can be used to identify you in a photo of a large crowd.

Al Franken

If you use a cell phone - as I do - your wireless carrier likely has records about your physical movements going back months, if not years.

Al Franken

If you want a free email service that doesn't use your words to target ads to you, you'll have to figure out how to port years and years of Gmail messages somewhere else, which is about as easy as developing your own free email service.

Al Franken

In my first week as a U.S. senator, I had the privilege of participating in the Supreme Court confirmation hearing for Judge Sonia Sotomayor.

Al Franken

In our political system, money is power. And that means a few can have a lot more power than the rest. That's bad news for everyone else - and for our democracy itself.

Al Franken

It is my fondest wish that in the fullness of time, the American people will look back on the Franken presidency as something of a mixed bag and not as a complete disaster.

Al Franken

It's easier to put on slippers than to carpet the whole world.

Al Franken

It's hard for a liberal to go on between Sean Hannity and Rush Limbaugh, because it's like doing country music after hip-hop. I mean, just, the audience doesn't go from one to the other.

Al Franken

It's hard to have that debate around secret programs authorized by secret legal opinions issued by a secret court. Actually, it's impossible to have that debate.

Al Franken

It's the Power of the Almighty, the Splendor of Nature, and then you.

Al Franken

Let's keep the Internet weird. Let's keep the Internet free.

Al Franken

Let's not let the government sell us out. Let's fight for net neutrality.

Al Franken

Liberals like me love America. We just love America in a different way.

Al Franken

Minnesota has a proud tradition of having two Senators on the Ag committee - a tradition I'd like very much to continue.

Al Franken

Minnesotans know the difference between the job of satirist and the job of senator. And so do I.

Al Franken

Minnesotans lost their jobs because the credit rating agencies didn't do the only job they're supposed to have, the only job they had, which is to give accurate, objective ratings to financial products.

Al Franken

Mistakes are a part of being human. Appreciate your mistakes for what they are: precious life lessons that can only be learned the hard way. Unless it's a fatal mistake, which, at least, others can learn from.

Al Franken

Most Americans don't think about antitrust law when they look at their cable bill, flip channels on TV, or worry about what their favorite website knows about them. But they should.

Al Franken

My dad always told me to stand up to bullies, and Bill O'Reilly is kind of a bully, and he's the kind of kid who hits other kids on the playground. And when you hit him, he runs to the teacher and says, 'Teacher, sue him.'

Al Franken

My dad didn't graduate from high school, ended up being a printing salesman, probably never made more than $8,000 a year. My mom sold real estate and did it part time.

Al Franken

My dad loved comedians, especially George Jessel, and he loved Henny Youngman and Buddy Hackett.

Al Franken

My dad never graduated high school. He was a printing salesman. We lived in a two-bedroom, one-bath house in St. Louis Park, Minnesota. We weren't rich - but we felt secure.

Al Franken

My dad was a terrible businessman.

Al Franken

My daughter became a teacher right out of college.

Al Franken

My parents didn't make a lot of money. My dad was not a high school graduate - he didn't have a career as such; he was a printing salesman essentially for most of his working life.

Al Franken

My parents were really political. The news was very important in our home. We basically had dinner every night while watching the news, and then we'd discuss it with our parents.

Al Franken

My spiritual life is... sometimes I have access to it and sometimes I don't. When I do have access to it, it's usually a sense of my understanding what the best course of action or the best thing for me to do. By best, I mean when I have a real sense of doing the right thing and doing good for people and the connected universe of everybody.

Al Franken

My views about God come from my dad. Dad told me that he believed Nature, which to him included humankind, to be so beautiful, so magnificent, that there had to be something behind it all.

Al Franken

National security laws must protect national security. But they must also protect the public trust and preserve the ability of an informed electorate to hold its government to account.

Al Franken

Net neutrality has been in place since the very beginning of the Internet.

Al Franken

Net neutrality isn't a government takeover of the Internet, as many of my Republican colleagues have alleged.

Al Franken

No one is more sensitive to the issue of overeating than the creator of Stuart Smalley.

Al Franken

Our laws need to reflect the evolution of technology and the changing expectations of American society. This is why the Constitution is often called a 'living' document.

Al Franken

Part of the middle class promise is that, after a lifetime of hard work, you'll be able to retire and enjoy the fruits of that labor. Medicare was established to secure that promise.

Al Franken

People lucky enough to live in the vicinity of an industrial hog farm are, with each breath, made keenly aware of the cause of their declining property values.

Al Franken

Progressives, in a way, are the new conservatives. We want to conserve what we fought to build.

Al Franken

Ralph Nader is a hero. I know Ralph, and I call him up occasionally. He's helped me out on a couple of occasions when I've given speeches to corporations where he'd have a good... He'd give me some good information.

Al Franken

Service dogs raise their masters' sense of well-being.

Al Franken

Small businesses should have the same ability to reach customers as powerful corporations. A blogger should have the same ability to find an audience as a media conglomerate.

Al Franken

Some of George W. Bush's friends say that Bush believes God called him to be president during these times of trial. But God told me that He/She/It had actually chosen Al Gore by making sure that Gore won the popular vote and, God thought, the Electoral College. 'That worked for everyone else,' God said.

Al Franken

Some of my colleagues seem more interested in using every procedural method possible to keep the Senate from doing anything than they are in creating jobs or helping Americans struggling in a difficult economy.

Al Franken

Sometimes if I tell people, 'I'm afraid that I'm really a fraud,' or 'I have a lot of self-doubt,' they go, 'Oh, no, you're kidding.' I go, 'No, I'm really honest.'

Al Franken

Technology is an incredible tool - it connects people to each other, creates jobs all over the world, and makes life easier for millions of Americans.

Al Franken

Teen pregnancy went way down in the '90s, and 75 percent of it was because of increased use of contraception.

Al Franken

Terrorism, to me, is the use of terror for political purpose, and terror is indiscriminate murder of civilians to make a political point.

Al Franken

The Founders who crafted our Constitution and Bill of Rights were careful to draft a Constitution of limited powers - one that would protect Americans' liberty at all times - both in war, and in peace.

Al Franken

The Fourth Amendment doesn't apply to corporations.

Al Franken

The Medicare Part D prescription drug bill, which might be the most corrupt piece of legislation in history, was a huge giveaway of taxpayer funds to the big pharmaceutical companies.

Al Franken

The Minnesotans I talk to are really concerned about what the future holds for their families. They're trying to pay for health care and send their kids to college, they're worried about declining home values, they're scared for a loved one they have serving in Iraq.

Al Franken

The Republican agenda is a radical vision in which Medicaid is slashed to the bone - in which we start to balance the budget on the backs of, literally, our most vulnerable citizens.

Al Franken

The biases the media has are much bigger than conservative or liberal. They're about getting ratings, about making money, about doing stories that are easy to cover.

Al Franken

The civil rights movement was very important in my house, and then Vietnam was very important 'cause there were two boys, so I came of age during a very heated political climate.

Al Franken

The government must give proper weight to both keeping America safe from terrorists and protecting Americans' privacy. But when Americans lack the most basic information about our domestic surveillance programs, they have no way of knowing whether we're getting that balance right. This lack of transparency is a big problem.

Al Franken

The institutions that we've built up over the years to protect our individual privacy rights from the government don't apply to the private sector. The Fourth Amendment doesn't apply to corporations. The Freedom of Information Act doesn't apply to Silicon Valley. And you can't impeach Google if it breaks its 'Don't be evil' campaign pledge.

Al Franken

The nature of the Internet and the importance of net neutrality is that innovation can come from everyone.

Al Franken

The next thing I am doing is moving back home to Minnesota and getting involved in politics. I'm looking at a run for Senate in 2008, but in the meantime I am focused on knitting together the progressive network in the upper Midwest.

Al Franken

The point is that there is tremendous hypocrisy among the Christian right. And I think that Christian voters should start looking at global warming and extreme poverty as a religious issue that speaks to the culture of life.

Al Franken

The reason I wrote political satire was because I thought it - politics - was important... that public policy was important. Then I transitioned into books, then into radio.

Al Franken

The right wing has had a radio apparatus for years and years, so they've had minor leagues - they've had local rightwing guys who've become national rightwing guys, and who build slowly, and that's how it goes. We haven't had that. It isn't like we have a farm team.

Al Franken

The thing that interests me least about the radio business is the radio business. But I've had to learn a little bit about it. It's not rocket science: You get ratings, that's good.

Al Franken

The way I see it, I'm not going to Washington to be the 60th Democratic senator. I'm going to Washington to be the second senator from the state of Minnesota.

Al Franken

There is - I mean - I found early in life that righteous indignation is a little off-putting, and so I try to couch it with humor.

Al Franken

There is a subset of Democrats who tend to mis-fill out ballots. The way you mark the ballot is like an S.A.T. - you fill in the circle. And the subset of people who tend to, like, put a check there instead, or an X, or fill it out wrong, tend to be people who didn't take S.A.T.s, or first-time voters, or people with English as a second language.

Al Franken

There's an appeal to the American sense of exceptionalism, that we're morally superior, as way to not be self-critical. I think that's a bit dangerous.

Al Franken

There's no comparison between NPR and the propaganda that you hear from Rush or from Sean Hannity, the news movement conservatives that are just laying out, slathering out the disinformation and the lies, as I discuss in my book, 'Lies and the Lying Liars Who Tell Them: A Fair and Balanced Look at the Right.'

Al Franken

There's plenty of room for humor in politics, God knows, but it's a serious business.

Al Franken

To ask whether the mainstream media has a conservative or liberal bias is like asking whether al-Qaida uses too much oil in their hummus. It's - I think they might use too much oil in their hummus - but it's the wrong question.

Al Franken

To make the argument that the media has a left- or right-wing, or a liberal or a conservative bias, is like asking if the problem with Al-Qaeda is do they use too much oil in their hummus.

Al Franken

Too many people don't protect their smartphones with a password or PIN. I anticipate that Apple's fingerprint reader will in fact make iPhone 5S owners more likely to secure their smartphones.

Al Franken

Veterans report that service dogs help break their isolation. People will often avert their eyes when they see a wounded veteran. But when the veteran has a dog, the same people will come up and say, 'Hi' to pet the dog and then strike up a conversation.

Al Franken

We need to prepare our kids for a 21st Century economy, and we're not doing it with our schools.

Al Franken

We need to start by having a conversation about climate change. It would be irresponsible to avoid the issue just because it's uncomfortable to talk about.

Al Franken

We owe an historic debt to American Indians. They have a unique set of concerns that haven't been addressed, and I'd like to stand with them. Also, I'd like to get their views on immigration.

Al Franken

Well, a lot of politics is communicating with people, and obviously comedy has something to do with that. I've been a producer and led people. Also, being a comedian, you're under pressure.

Al Franken

What you see on the campaign trail is me. It's easy being me.

Al Franken

When I first started writing for television in the seventies and eighties, the Internet didn't exist, and we didn't need to worry about foreign websites illegally distributing the latest TV shows and blockbuster movies online.

Al Franken

When a company is able to establish a dominant market position, consumers lose meaningful choices. You might not like that Facebook shares your political opinions with Politico, but are you really going to delete all the photos, all the posts, all the connections - the presence you've spent years establishing on the world's dominant social network?

Al Franken

When people talked about protecting their privacy when I was growing up, they were talking about protecting it from the government. They talked about unreasonable searches and seizures, about keeping the government out of their bedrooms.

Al Franken

When the Constitution was written, the founders had no way of anticipating the new technologies that would evolve in the coming centuries.

Al Franken

When the president during the campaign said he was against nation building, I didn't realize he meant our nation.

Al Franken

When you encounter seemingly good advice that contradicts other seemingly good advice, ignore them both.

Al Franken

When you live in New York, one of two things happen - you either become a New Yorker, or you feel more like the place you came from.

Al Franken

When you win an election, what you really win is a chance to go to work for working families who need a voice in Minnesota.

Al Franken

Why don't we focus on what Afghan women can do? They can cook, bear children and pray. As I recall, that was fine for our grandmothers.

Al Franken

Yeah, but you need an experienced radio veteran who is a liberal advocate. And there just hadn't been any radio that did that. And so they weren't trained - they had developed all these bad habits of being objective and balanced and stuff like that.

Al Franken

Yeah, we shot ourselves in the foot right out of the gate. The guy who ran it at first misled pretty much everybody about how much capital we had. He said we had enough to go three years without making money, and we had enough to go three weeks.

Al Franken

You can't change your fingerprints. You have only ten of them. And you leave them on everything you touch; they are definitely not a secret.

Al Franken

You have to love your country like an adult loves somebody, not like a child loves its mommy. And right-wing Republicans tend to love America like a child loves its mommy, where everything Mommy does is okay. But adult love means you're not in denial, and you want the loved one to be the best they can be.

Al Franken

You know, Lincoln was funny. I don't think F.D.R. was very funny. But Lincoln was funny. Lincoln was really funny. But I think you should get elected first, and then show that you're funny.

Al Franken

You might not like that Facebook shares your political opinions with Politico, but are you really going to delete all the photos, all the posts, all the connections - the presence you've spent years establishing on the world's dominant social network?

Al Franken

This page is intentionally left blank

This page is intentionally left blank

This page is intentionally left blank

This page is intentionally left blank

This page is intentionally left blank

www.ingramcontent.com/pod-product-compliance
Lightning Source LLC
Chambersburg PA
CBHW071144280526
45787CB00003B/1397